Bes

Ancient Protector & Nightmare Deflector

WRITTEN BY
SHELLI WRIGHT JOHNSON

ILLUSTRATED BY
SCOTTY ROBERTS

Bes
Ancient Protector & Nightmare Deflector

ISBN: 978-0-9987236-1-7

Published by

www.BesPress.com
USA

Cover, Illustrations & Interior design by Scotty Roberts www.scottalanroberts.com

Printed in the United States of America

Dedication

For
John Anthony West
who introduced me to ancient Egypt's pint-sized hero,
and encouraged me to put pen to paper....

Bes

Ancient Protector & Nightmare Deflector

Bowie was an adventurer,
bold and brave by day.
It was only in the night time
that his courage went away.

The beasts that he would battle
so fiercely in the light,
would often come to taunt him
in the middle of the night.

He'd toss and turn for hours
imagining monsters 'round his bed,
tugging tightly on the blanket
as he covered up his head.

Oh, he'd try to put his mind at rest
and find a bit of peace,
but Bo could count a thousand sheep
and still not fall asleep.

Then one dark and stormy night
(the kind that monsters like the best),
shadows danced across the dresser,
heartbeats echoed in his chest. . .

He wondered what sorts of beasties
were looming in that gloom.
Perhaps the usual suspects
were already hiding in his room.

(The biggest dread while in his bed
was pondering which creature
would present itself for duty
as that evening's nightmare feature).

So, imagine Bowie's reaction
when he began his nightly scan,
and spotted a funky feathered headdress
crowning a bluish little man!!!

YIKES! – What kind of creature was this?
Was he friend or foe?
Bo ducked beneath the blanket.
It was just too soon to know.

From deep under the covers
he pondered his fate . . .
Was this just a bad dream?
Was it something he ate?

Had his over-active imagination
suddenly gone 'round the bend?
Was this some practical joke?
Was it all just pretend?

But when he dared sneak a peek,
the little man was still there.
Living . . . Breathing . . .
And returning his stare!!

This was wholly unexpected.
Bo didn't know what to do,
so he began to search for anything
that might give him a clue . . .

He spied a bushy beard curling
round a face old and crinkled,
and a bold V-shaped brow
framing dark eyes that twinkled . . .

A stubby body draped in leopard,
belted with a real live snake —
OH! The gnarly imp stuck out his tongue,
causing Bowie's hands to shake.

My name is Bes. I'm here to help,
the wee man casually declared.
Poor Bowie found he couldn't speak
because he was just too scared!

You see, Bowie's chin was wagging,
but his words wouldn't work.
Bes rolled his dark eyes,
then grinned, with a smirk.

Though this "Bes" was bizarre,
his intentions seemed fine,
so Bowie gathered the gumption
for his opening line:

6

"You're here – to – help – what?"
he asked, still trembling with fright.
I'm here to chase away things
that go bump in the night.

(Just when it seemed that
things couldn't get stranger –
the pint-sized visitor had claimed
he could vanquish all danger!)

Bowie found himself staring
at the imp's lolling tongue . . .
Lucky for you, I arrived
while the night is still young.

You see, I've been around forever.
I know the monsters by name.
I watch over the children
and turn those nasty beasts tame.

So, what's bothering you, boy?
This room looks quite clear.
There's no sign of trouble
lurking anywhere near.

Bowie looked up and down –
sizing up his new guest.
The blue man talked a good game,
but Bo remained unimpressed.

"You seem . . . um . . . a mite [gulp] short
to chase monsters away.
What about the Boogeyman?
Can you keep him at bay?"

Ba! I may be small,
but my powers are strong.
Consider him vanished, banished
and most permanently gone.

"But I think I heard a goblin
say I was ripe for the pickin'."
Why, I'll crunch him and munch him.
They taste just like chicken.

"Over there . . . by the window –
is that is a big hungry bear?"
I'll feed him and lead him
right out the back stair.

"What if I saw a green Martian
with big eyes on its face?"
I'll sock it and rocket it
back into space.

"And that shrew in my shoe
with a glowing red eye?"
I'll scold it and blindfold it.
Just as easy as pie.

"There's a dusty ol' mummy
who visits quite often."
*I'll re-wrap it and zap it
right back to its coffin.*

*Mummies are my speciality.
We've a lot of them at home.
In Egypt, they're as common
as your everyday yard gnome.*

"Oh! Is that a pirate
peeking out from the hamper?"
*YAR . . I'll sing him to sleep
and sling him into the camper.*

"There's a lion in the bathroom –
maybe a gorilla, or two."
*I'll bag 'em and tag 'em,
and ship 'em back to the zoo.*

"Look! I think that's a bat
hanging there on the ceiling."
*I'll wake it and shake it
and send it off squealing.*

"And that sabertooth tiger
who hasn't eaten all day?"
*I'll spank it and thank it
to be on its way.*

There is nothing to fear.
You have nothing to dread . . .
The stuff of your nightmares
is all in your head.

"Is that a ghost hovering
up high in the air?"
It's only the wind.
Nothing else is up there.

"Well, the thunder is banging
and the lightning is flashing–"
And you're safe in your room.
It's the outside that's bashing.

"But it's so dark in here . . .
things seem scary and creepy."
No need to fear that,
Just relax . . . Aren't you sleepy?

You see this big staff?
It has powerful magic.
It can protect against things
that are otherwise tragic.

"What about that ogre in the closet
who won't stop yackin'?"
I'll gag him and bag him,
and send him off packin'.

"Can it stop a thirsty vampire
from biting on my neck?"
I'll pull that fang and let it hang.
One less monster. Check ✓

"That wicked witch on her broomstick,
with the bumpy green face?"
Watch me sweep her and keep her
from bothering this place.

"And those weird-looking paw-prints
leading in from the street?"
No worries there, boy.
Those are just from my feet.

Hmmm . . . Do you have any experience?"
Bowie asked without guilt.
Why, I started doing this work
before the pyramids were built!

I was the first action hero –
ancient Egypt's most powerful elf.
And I still pack quite a punch,
if I do say so myself.

You see . . . I chased off the demons
that bothered King Tut.
I watched over young Horus,
and the sky-goddess Nut.

I'm the 'Guardian against Nightmares.'
I banish night beasts to cages.
Protecting folks from bad dreams?
I've been doing it for ages.

Watch – I roll out my tongue
and the monsters take heed.
I hold out my staff,
they pick up the speed.

And so, Master Bowie,
there is no need to fear.
The beasties keep their distance
because they know I'm here.

"Okay . . . But did you see that?
I think I saw something scurry– "
It's only a shadow.
There's no need to worry.

"But what if Bigfoot
should come looking for me?"
We'll pull up a chair
and invite him to tea.

Shhh. . . No more creatures.
I'll protect you, **Bes said.**
Close your eyes, and your mouth,
and just lie back in bed.

Now, think good thoughts
and wipe off that frown.
Nothing's gonna harm you —
not while I'm around.

"I am getting sleepy,
but what if I find–"
Just shoosh it and push it
right out of your mind.

Bowie smiled, then yawned,
returning Bes's big grin.
He was feeling much better
since his guest had come in.

And then there was quiet,
the list had come to an end.
Bo knew not to worry;
he trusted his friend.

Bes adjusted the covers
on Bowie's small bed,
and gently planted a kiss
a'top the boy's head.

There were no more monsters
to be had on that night.
Bowie was dreaming . . .
Bes turned out the light.

Good night, young prince.
Dream well and sleep tight.
No need to worry . . .
I'll be here all night.

ABOUT BES . . .

Stubby and full-faced, this under-sized and over-stuffed member of the ancient Egyptian pantheon is easily recognized by his feathered headdress and protruding tongue. Because he was believed to ward off all manner of misfortune, Bes was long celebrated as "Champion of Everything Good and Defender against Everything Bad." *Way to go, Bes!*

Bes had many duties, including guardian against nightmares and dangerous creatures of the night. Likenesses of Bes, poised and ready to chase away any nasty night-beasts that might come calling, can still be seen decorating the bed and headrest of Egypt's famous boy-king, Tutankhamen . . . Did you know that in ancient times, mothers would draw a likeness of Bes on the palm of their child's left hand at bedtime, then wrap that hand in linen to activate the protective powers of this fierce little guardian? You may want to try this the next time you have trouble sleeping.

Hello, Bes. Good bye, nightmares!

You can learn more about Bes, and find other books about this pint-sized hero of old at **www.bespress.com**.

24

www.ingramcontent.com/pod-product-compliance
Lightning Source LLC
Chambersburg PA
CBHW040022050426
42452CB00002B/96